JAZZ PLAY ALONG

Book and CD for B♭, E♭ and C Instruments

**Arranged and Produced by
Mark Taylor**

The Blues
10 BLUES CLASSICS

TITLE	PAGE NUMBERS			
	C Treble Instruments	B♭ Instruments	E♭ Instruments	C Bass Instruments
Billie's Bounce	4	14	24	34
Birk's Works	5	15	25	35
Blues for Alice	6	16	26	36
Blues In The Closet	7	17	27	37
C-Jam Blues	8	18	28	38
Freddie Freeloader	9	19	29	39
Mr. P.C.	10	20	30	40
Now's The Time	11	21	31	41
Tenor Madness	12	22	32	42
Things Ain't What They Used To Be	13	23	33	43

TITLE	CD Track Number Split Track / Melody	CD Track Number Full Stereo Track
Billie's Bounce	1	2
Birk's Works	3	4
Blues for Alice	5	6
Blues In The Closet	7	8
C-Jam Blue	9	10
Freddie Freeloader	11	12
Mr. P.C.	13	14
Now's The Time	15	16
Tenor Madness	17	18
Things Ain't What They Used To Be	19	20
B♭ Tuning Notes		21

ISBN 978-0-634-03917-1

**HAL•LEONARD®
CORPORATION**
7777 W. BLUEMOUND RD. P.O. BOX 13819 MILWAUKEE, WI 53213

Visit Hal Leonard Online at
www.halleonard.com

The Blues

Arranged and Produced by
Mark Taylor

Featured Players:

Joseph Henson-Tenor Sax
John Desalme-Tenor Sax
Tony Nalker-Piano
Jim Roberts-Bass
Steve Fidyk-Drums

HOW TO USE THE CD:

Each song has two tracks:

1) Split Track/Melody

Woodwind, Brass, Keyboard, and Mallet Players can use this track as a learning tool for melody style and inflection.

Bass Players can learn and perform with this track – remove the recorded bass track by turning down the volume on the LEFT channel.

Keyboard and **Guitar Players** can learn and perform with this track – remove the recorded piano part by turning down the volume on the RIGHT channel.

2) Full Stereo Track

Soloists or **groups** can learn and perform with this accompaniment track with the RHYTHM SECTION only.

BILLIE'S BOUNCE

C VERSION

BY CHARLIE PARKER

BIRK'S WORKS

BY DIZZY GILLESPIE

C VERSION

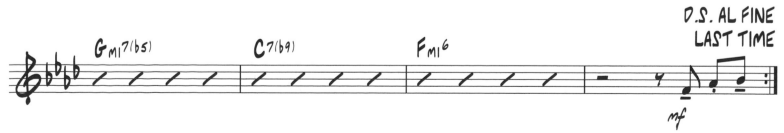

BLUES FOR ALICE

CD
5: Split Track/Melody
6: Full Stereo Track

C VERSION

BY CHARLIE PARKER

BLUES IN THE CLOSET

CD

7 : Split Track/Melody

8 : Full Stereo Track

C VERSION

BY OSCAR PETTIFORD

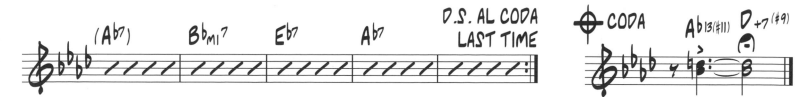

C-JAM BLUES

CD
9 : Split Track/Melody
10 : Full Stereo Track

C VERSION

BY DUKE ELLINGTON

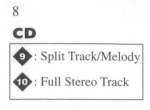

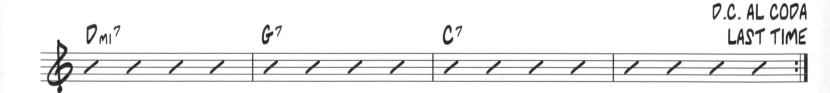

FREDDIE FREELOADER

CD
11 : Split Track/Melody
12 : Full Stereo Track

C VERSION

BY MILES DAVIS

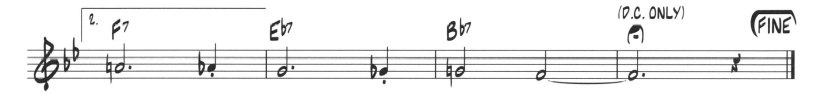

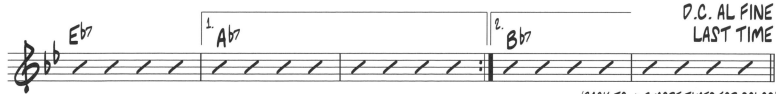

(BACK TO * 3 MORE TIMES FOR SOLOS)

CD

◆ **13** : Split Track/Melody

◆ **14** : Full Stereo Track

MR. P.C.

C VERSION

BY JOHN COLTRANE

NOW'S THE TIME

CD
15 : Split Track/Melody
16 : Full Stereo Track

C VERSION

BY CHARLIE PARKER

TENOR MADNESS

C VERSION

BY SONNY ROLLINS

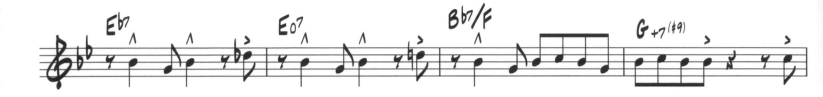

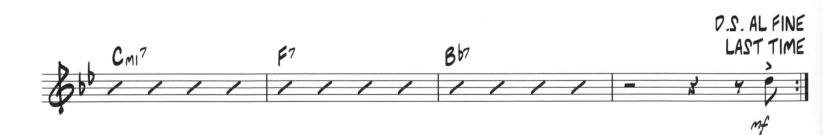

CD
◆ **19** : Split Track/Melody
◆ **20** : Full Stereo Track

THINGS AIN'T WHAT THEY USED TO BE

C VERSION

BY MERCER ELLINGTON

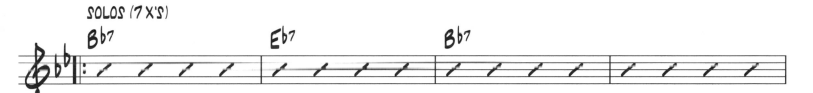

CD

◆1 : Split Track/Melody

◆2 : Full Stereo Track

BILLIE'S BOUNCE

BY CHARLIE PARKER

B♭ VERSION

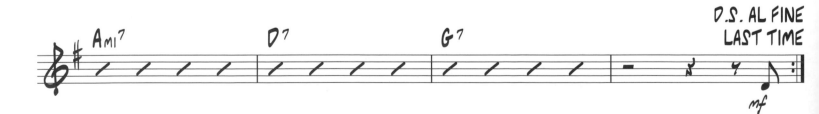

CD

◆3 : Split Track/Melody
◆4 : Full Stereo Track

BIRK'S WORKS

B♭ VERSION

BY DIZZY GILLESPIE

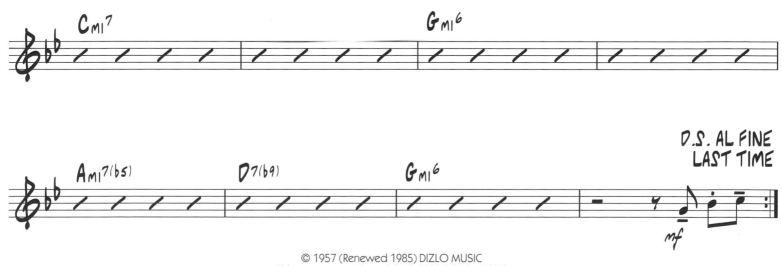

BLUES FOR ALICE

CD
5 : Split Track/Melody
6 : Full Stereo Track

Bb Version

BY CHARLIE PARKER

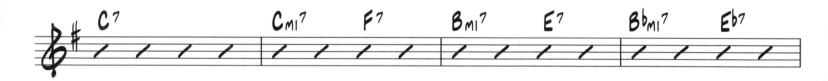

BLUES IN THE CLOSET

BY OSCAR PETTIFORD

Bb VERSION

SWING!

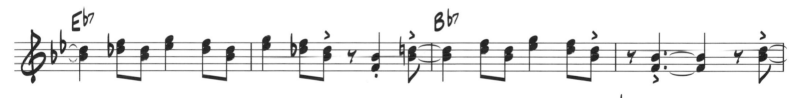

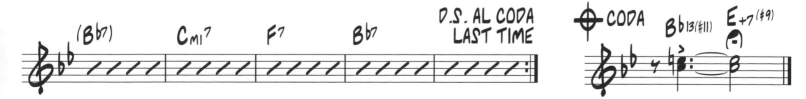

CD
9 : Split Track/Melody
10 : Full Stereo Track

C-Jam Blues

$B\flat$ VERSION

BY DUKE ELLINGTON

CD
11 : Split Track/Melody
12 : Full Stereo Track

FREDDIE FREELOADER

BY MILES DAVIS

Bb VERSION

MEDIUM SWING

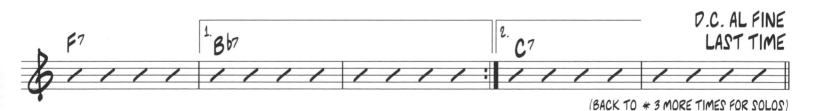

D.C. AL FINE
LAST TIME

(BACK TO ＊ 3 MORE TIMES FOR SOLOS)

MR. P.C.

CD
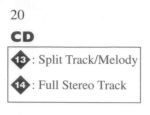
🔷 : Split Track/Melody
🔷 : Full Stereo Track

Bb VERSION

BY JOHN COLTRANE

NOW'S THE TIME

CD
15 : Split Track/Melody
16 : Full Stereo Track

B♭ VERSION

BY CHARLIE PARKER

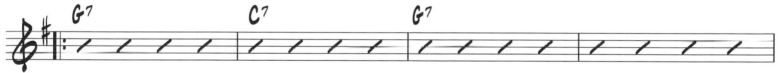

TENOR MADNESS

CD

◆**17** : Split Track/Melody
◆**18** : Full Stereo Track

Bᵇ VERSION

BY SONNY ROLLINS

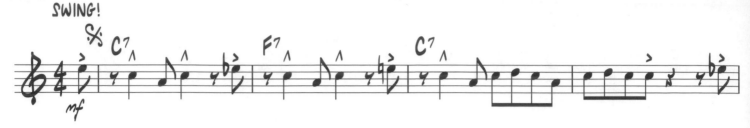

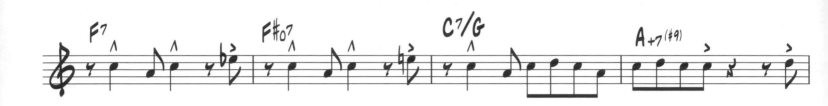

SOLOS (9X'S)

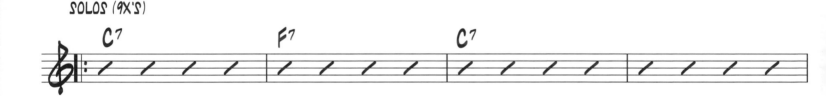

D.S. AL FINE
LAST TIME

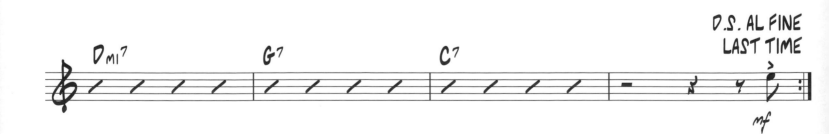

THINGS AIN'T WHAT THEY USED TO BE

CD
◆ **19** : Split Track/Melody
◆ **20** : Full Stereo Track

Bb VERSION

BY MERCER ELLINGTON

BILLIE'S BOUNCE

CD

1 : Split Track/Melody
2 : Full Stereo Track

Eb VERSION

BY CHARLIE PARKER

SOLOS (10X'S)

D.S. AL FINE
LAST TIME

CD
3 : Split Track/Melody
4 : Full Stereo Track

BIRK'S WORKS

Eb VERSION

BY DIZZY GILLESPIE

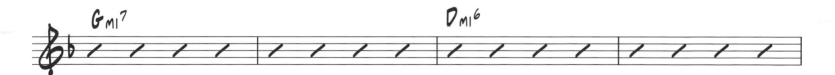

CD
5 : Split Track/Melody
6 : Full Stereo Track

BLUES FOR ALICE

BY CHARLIE PARKER

E♭ VERSION

CD

BLUES IN THE CLOSET

By Oscar Pettiford

E♭ VERSION

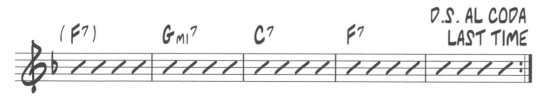

CD
◆ 9 : Split Track/Melody
◆ 10 : Full Stereo Track

C-Jam Blues

Eb VERSION

BY DUKE ELLINGTON

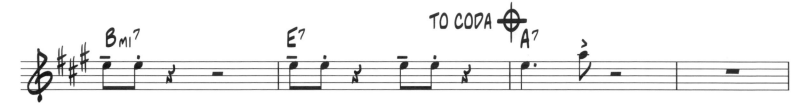

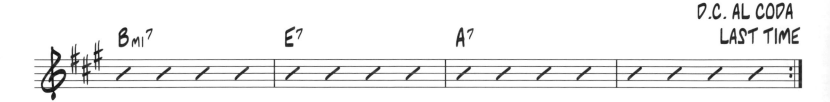

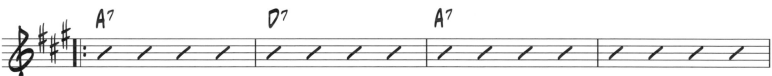

FREDDIE FREELOADER

BY MILES DAVIS

Eb VERSION

(BACK TO ✳ 3 MORE TIMES FOR SOLOS)

CD
13 : Split Track/Melody
14 : Full Stereo Track

MR. P.C.

E♭ VERSION

BY JOHN COLTRANE

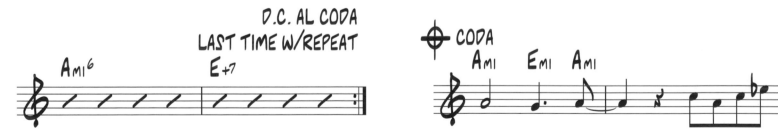

NOW'S THE TIME

CD
15 : Split Track/Melody
16 : Full Stereo Track

BY CHARLIE PARKER

Eb VERSION

TENOR MADNESS

E♭ VERSION

BY SONNY ROLLINS

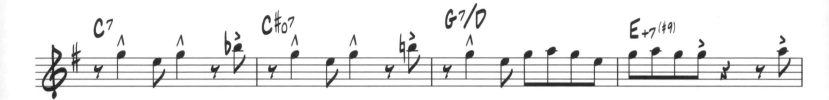

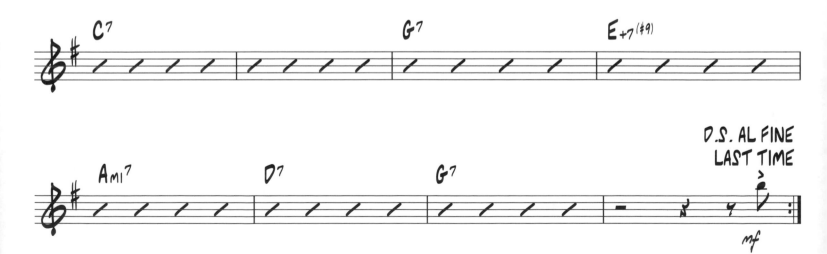

THINGS AIN'T WHAT THEY USED TO BE

CD
19: Split Track/Melody
20: Full Stereo Track

BY MERCER ELLINGTON

E♭ VERSION

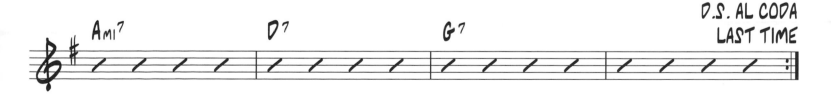

CD

1 : Split Track/Melody
2 : Full Stereo Track

BILLIE'S BOUNCE

BY CHARLIE PARKER

C VERSION

BRIGHT SWING

SOLOS (10X'S)

D.S. AL FINE
LAST TIME

CD
3 : Split Track/Melody
4 : Full Stereo Track

BIRK'S WORKS

BY DIZZY GILLESPIE

𝄢: C VERSION

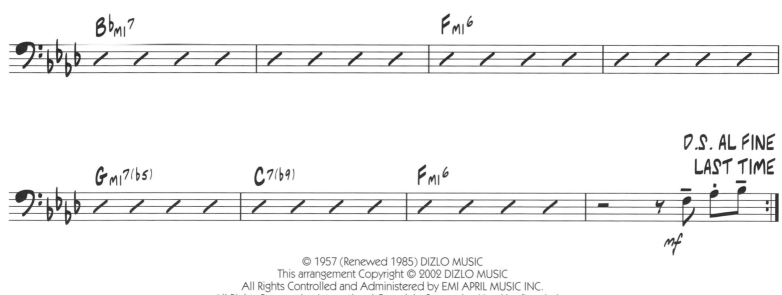

BLUES FOR ALICE

BY CHARLIE PARKER

9: C VERSION

CD

7 : Split Track/Melody
8 : Full Stereo Track

BLUES IN THE CLOSET

BY OSCAR PETTIFORD

𝄢: C VERSION

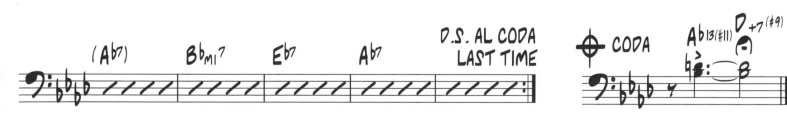

C-JAM BLUES

BY DUKE ELLINGTON

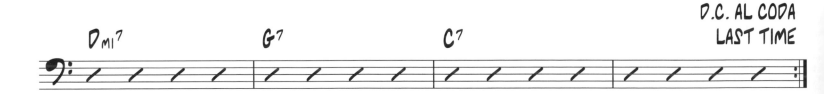

FREDDIE FREELOADER

BY MILES DAVIS

CD
- 🔺 : Split Track/Melody
- ◆12 : Full Stereo Track

♪: C VERSION

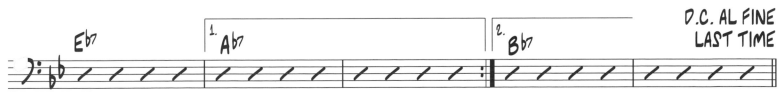

(BACK TO ✱ 3 MORE TIMES FOR SOLOS)

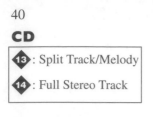

MR. P.C.

BY JOHN COLTRANE

9: C VERSION

NOW'S THE TIME

BY CHARLIE PARKER

⑨: C VERSION

TENOR MADNESS

BY SONNY ROLLINS

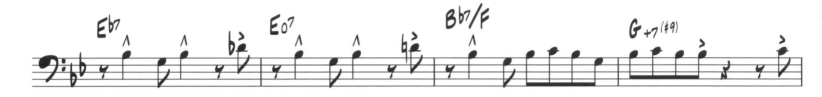

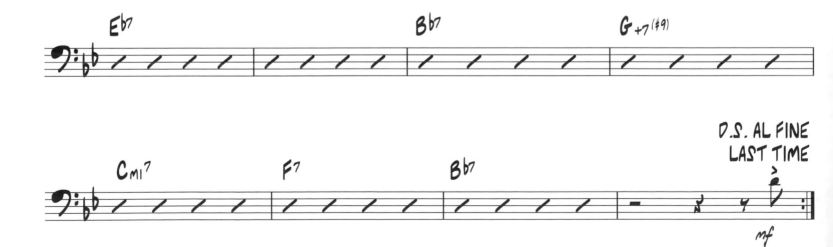

CD
19 : Split Track/Melody
20 : Full Stereo Track

THINGS AIN'T WHAT THEY USED TO BE

BY MERCER ELLINGTON

𝄢: C VERSION

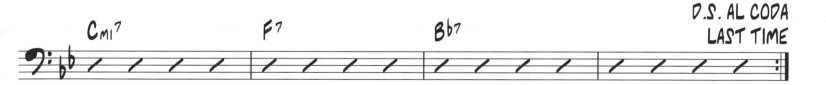

For use with all B-flat, E-flat, Bass Clef and C instruments, the Jazz Play-Along® Series is the ultimate learning tool for all jazz musicians. With musician-friendly lead sheets, melody cues, and other split-track audio choices included, these first-of-a-kind packages help you master improvisation while playing some of the greatest tunes of all time. FOR STUDY, each tune includes a split track with: melody cue with proper style and inflection • professional rhythm tracks • choruses for soloing • removable bass part • removable piano part. FOR PERFORMANCE, each tune also has: an additional full stereo accompaniment track (no melody) • additional choruses for soloing.

1A. MAIDEN VOYAGE/ALL BLUES
00843158 .... $15.99

1. DUKE ELLINGTON
00841644 .... $16.99

2. MILES DAVIS
00841645 .... $16.99

3. THE BLUES
00841646 .... $16.99

4. JAZZ BALLADS
00841691 .... $16.99

5. BEST OF BEBOP
00841689 .... $16.99

6. JAZZ CLASSICS WITH EASY CHANGES
00841690 .... $16.99

7. ESSENTIAL JAZZ STANDARDS
00843000 .... $16.99

8. ANTONIO CARLOS JOBIM AND THE ART OF THE BOSSA NOVA
00843001 .... $16.99

9. DIZZY GILLESPIE
00843002 .... $16.99

10. DISNEY CLASSICS
00843003 .... $16.99

12. ESSENTIAL JAZZ CLASSICS
00843005 .... $16.99

13. JOHN COLTRANE
00843006 .... $16.99

14. IRVING BERLIN
00843007 .... $16.99

15. RODGERS & HAMMERSTEIN
00843008 .... $16.99

16. COLE PORTER
00843009 .... $16.99

17. COUNT BASIE
00843010 .... $16.99

18. HAROLD ARLEN
00843011 .... $16.99

20. CHRISTMAS CAROLS
00843080 .... $16.99

21. RODGERS AND HART CLASSICS
00843014 .... $16.99

22. WAYNE SHORTER
00843015 .... $16.99

23. LATIN JAZZ
00843016 .... $16.99

24. EARLY JAZZ STANDARDS
00843017 .... $16.99

25. CHRISTMAS JAZZ
00843018 .... $16.99

26. CHARLIE PARKER
00843019 .... $16.99

27. GREAT JAZZ STANDARDS
00843020 .... $16.99

28. BIG BAND ERA
00843021 .... $16.99

29. LENNON AND MCCARTNEY
00843022 .... $16.99

30. BLUES' BEST
00843023 .... $16.99

31. JAZZ IN THREE
00843024 .... $16.99

32. BEST OF SWING
00843025 .... $17.99

33. SONNY ROLLINS
00843029 .... $16.99

34. ALL TIME STANDARDS
00843030 .... $16.99

35. BLUESY JAZZ
00843031 .... $16.99

36. HORACE SILVER
00843032 .... $16.99

37. BILL EVANS
00843033 .... $16.99

38. YULETIDE JAZZ
00843034 .... $16.99

39. "ALL THE THINGS YOU ARE" & MORE JEROME KERN SONGS
00843035 .... $16.99

40. BOSSA NOVA
00843036 .... $16.99

41. CLASSIC DUKE ELLINGTON
00843037 .... $16.99

42. GERRY MULLIGAN FAVORITES
00843038 .... $16.99

43. GERRY MULLIGAN CLASSICS
00843039 .... $16.99

45. GEORGE GERSHWIN
00103643 .... $24.99

47. CLASSIC JAZZ BALLADS
00843043 .... $16.99

48. BEBOP CLASSICS
00843044 .... $16.99

49. MILES DAVIS STANDARDS
00843045 .... $16.99

52. STEVIE WONDER
00843048 .... $16.99

53. RHYTHM CHANGES
00843049 .... $16.99

55. BENNY GOLSON
00843052 .... $16.99

56. "GEORGIA ON MY MIND" & OTHER SONGS BY HOAGY CARMICHAEL
00843056 .... $16.99

57. VINCE GUARALDI
00843057 .... $16.99

58. MORE LENNON AND MCCARTNEY
00843059 .... $16.99

59. SOUL JAZZ
00843060 .... $16.99

60. DEXTER GORDON
00843061 .... $16.99

61. MONGO SANTAMARIA
00843062 .... $16.99

62. JAZZ-ROCK FUSION
00843063 .... $16.99

63. CLASSICAL JAZZ
00843064 .... $16.99

64. TV TUNES
00843065 .... $16.99

65. SMOOTH JAZZ
00843066 .... $16.99

66. A CHARLIE BROWN CHRISTMAS
00843067 .... $16.99

67. CHICK COREA
00843068 .... $16.99

68. CHARLES MINGUS
00843069 .... $16.99

71. COLE PORTER CLASSICS
00843073 .... $16.99

72. CLASSIC JAZZ BALLADS
00843074 .... $16.99

73. JAZZ/BLUES
00843075 .... $16.99

74. BEST JAZZ CLASSICS
00843076 .... $16.99

75. PAUL DESMOND
00843077 .... $16.99

78. STEELY DAN
00843070 .... $16.99

79. MILES DAVIS CLASSICS
00843081 .... $16.99

80. JIMI HENDRIX
00843083 .... $16.99

83. ANDREW LLOYD WEBBER
00843104 .... $16.99

84. BOSSA NOVA CLASSICS
00843105 .... $16.99

85. MOTOWN HITS
00843109 .... $16.99

86. BENNY GOODMAN
00843110 .... $16.99

87. DIXIELAND
00843111 .... $16.99